# ABC BOOK of DOGS

by M.M. Linwe

Illustrated and designed by
Meradus Entertainment.

is for

# Akita

A furry coat to withstand the cold,
a fearless protector, strong and bold.

Pronunciation: ah·KEE·ta
Origin: Japan

Pronunciation: BRUH·suhls GRIFF·un
Origin: Belgium

# B

is for

# Brussels Griffon

Scaling heights with feline grace,
their one desire is your embrace.

# C

is for

# Cocker Spaniel

Their long and silky coat is a beautiful sight,
which comes in many colors from dark to light.

Pronunciation: KAH·ker SPAN·yuhl
Origin: England

Pronunciation: DAAKS·snd
Origin: Germany

# D

is for

# Dachshund

Like a hot dog, body long and low,
this pup is a dirt digging pro.

# E

is for

# English Bulldog

On a skateboard some can soar,
while others have a really loud snore.

Pronunciation: ING·glish BUL·dawg
Origin: England

Pronunciation: foks TER·ee·er
Origin: England

# F

is for

# Fox Terrier

Full of pep, they leap and bound,
chasing rodents on the ground.

# G

is for

# German Shepherd

Rescuing hearts, they are strong and kind,
a hero's soul, in them you'll find.

Pronunciation: GER·muhn SHEP·erd
Origin: Germany

Pronunciation: hav·uh·NEEZ
Origin: Cuba

# H

is for

# Havanese

Performing tricks, agility, and fun,
this playful lap dog is the one.

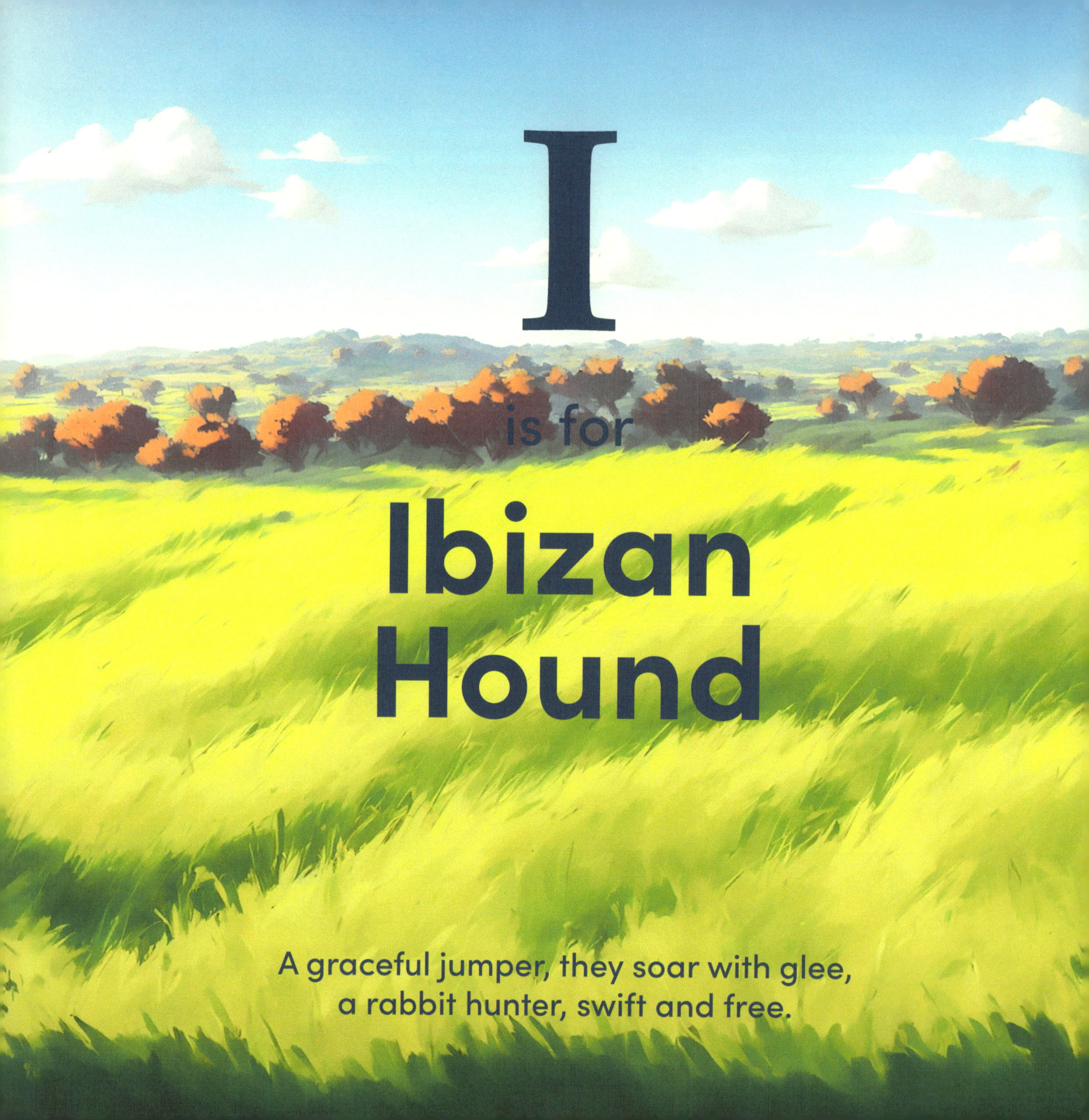

# I

is for

# Ibizan Hound

A graceful jumper, they soar with glee,
a rabbit hunter, swift and free.

Pronunciation: ih·BEE·zuhn HOWND
Origin: Spain

Pronunciation: jak·RUH·suhl TER·ee·er
Origin: England

# J

is for

# Jack Russell Terrier

With boundless joy, they fetch and run,
a playful pal, who's never done.

# K

is for

# Komondor

Corded locks, a guardian true,
this loyal friend watches sheep for you.

Pronunciation: KOM·uhn·dor
Origin: Hungary

Pronunciation: LAB·ruh·dor ree·TREEV·er
Origin: Canada

# L

is for

# Labrador Retriever

With love for water, they dive right in,
a joyful friend, a playful grin.

# M

## is for Maltese

Clever tricks and fur so bright,
this stunning dog is pure delight.

Pronunciation: mal·TEEZ
Origin: Malta

Pronunciation: NEW·fuhn·land
Origin: Canada

# N is for Newfoundland

Pulling carts with strength and speed,
and water rescues for those in need.

# O

is for

# Old English Sheepdog

Their family close they love to stay,
and guard the goats and sheep by day.

Pronunciation: old ING·glish SHEEP·dawg
Origin: England

Pronunciation: POOD·l
Origin: Germany

# P

is for

# Poodle

A curly coat and playful prance,
a brilliant mind and prideful stance.

is for

# Queensland Heeler

(Australian Cattle Dog)

Through hoops and tunnels they can dash,
at the heels of cows their teeth will nash.

Pronunciation: KWEEZ·land HEE·luhr
Origin: Australia

Pronunciation: roh·DEE·zhuhn RIJ·bak
Origin: Southern Africa

# R

is for

# Rhodesian Ridgeback

After lion and prey they sprint endlessly,
and for family they show great loyalty.

# S

is for

# Saluki

They chase gazelle with grace and speed,
an ancient heritage, the most regal breed.

Pronunciation: suh·LOO·kee
Origin: Middle East

Pronunciation: tih·BET·uhn MAS·tif
Origin: Tibet

# T

is for

# Tibetan Mastiff

A coat so warm, the cold won't bite,
a gentle guardian by day and night.

# U

is for

# Utonagan

The perfect playmate for any child,
though they look like a wolf from the wild.

Pronunciation: yoo·TON·uh·guhn
Origin: United Kingdom

Pronunciation: VEESH-luh
Origin: Hungary

# V

is for

# Vizsla

An athletic dog with a nose so keen,
they'll find lost game and things unseen.

# W

is for

# Whippet

It's a speedy race with rabbit in sight,
tired from the chase, they curl up so tight.

Pronunciation: WHIP·it
Origin: England

Pronunciation: show·loh·eets·KWEEN·tlee
Origin: Mexico

is for

# Xoloitzcuintli

(Xolo)

Once considered magical in times of old,
a statue warm to touch, hairless and bold.

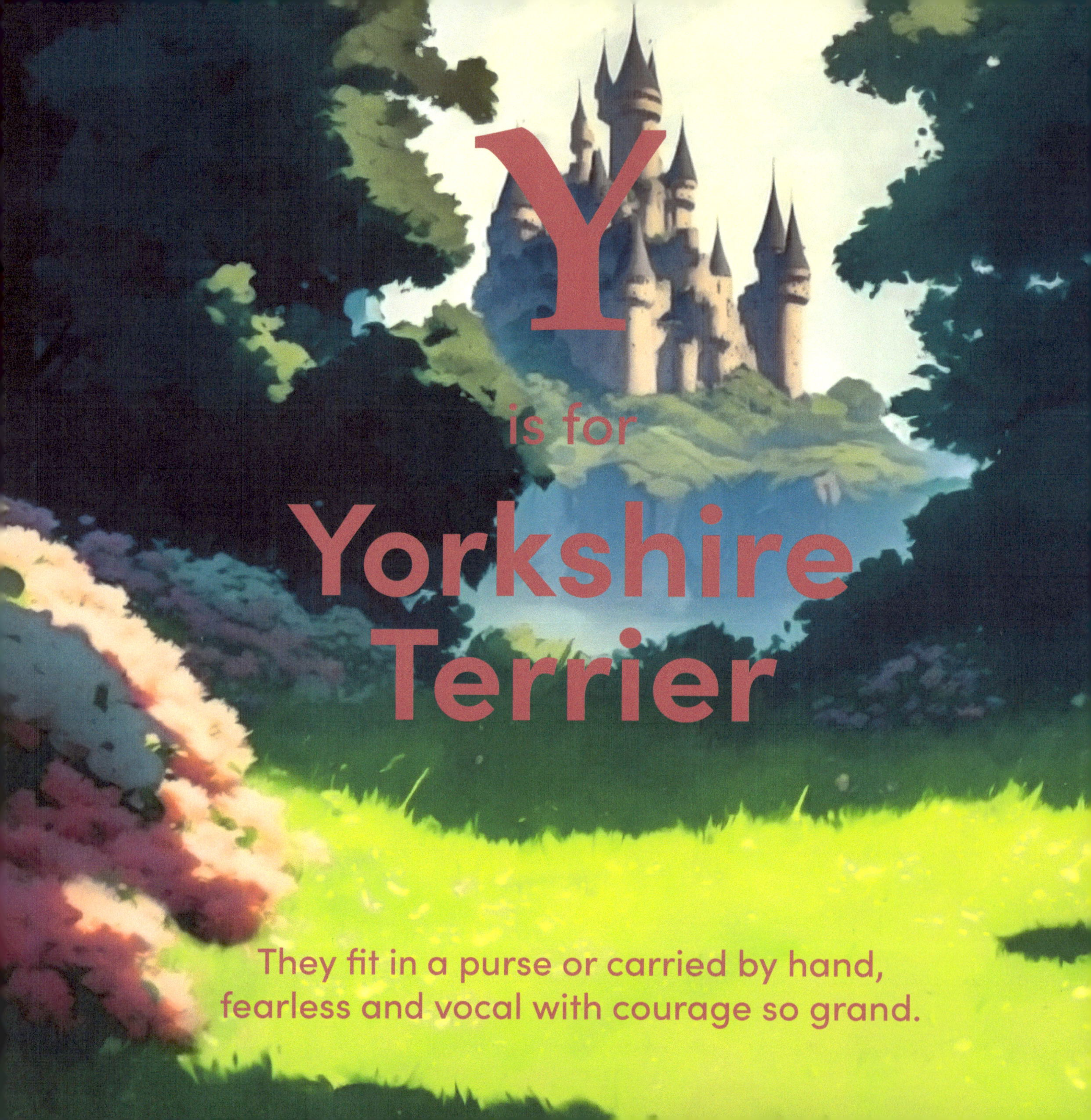

# Y

is for

# Yorkshire Terrier

They fit in a purse or carried by hand,
fearless and vocal with courage so grand.

Pronunciation: YORK·shur TER·ee·er
Origin: England

Pronunciation: ZVERG·shnow·zer
Origin: Germany

# Z

is for

# Zwergschnauzer

(Miniature Schnauzer)

This bearded face will stand its ground,
and keep your home safe and sound.